ROBERT CAPA

A FIREFLY BOOK

Published by Firefly Books Ltd. 2017

Original French-language edition copyright © 2016 Casterman
This English-language edition copyright © 2017 Firefly Books

First printing

Publisher Cataloging-in-Publication Data (U.S.)

Library of Congress Cataloging-in-Publication Data is available

Library and Archives Canada Cataloguing in Publication

Silloray, Florent
[Capa l'étoile filante. English]
    Robert Capa : a graphic biography / Florent Silloray.
Translation of: Capa l'étoile filante.
Includes bibliographical references.
ISBN 978-1-77085-928-9 (hardcover)
    1. Capa, Robert, 1913-1954–Comic books, strips, etc. 2. Photojournalists–
United States–Biography–Comic books, strips, etc. 3. War photographers–United
States–Biography– Comic books, strips, etc. 4. Comics (Graphic works) I. Title. II.
Title: Capa l'étoile filante. English
TR140.C28S55 2017   070.4'9092   C2017-901963-5

Published in the United States by
Firefly Books (U.S.) Inc.
P.O. Box 1338, Ellicott Station
Buffalo, New York 14205

Published in Canada by
Firefly Books Ltd.
50 Staples Avenue, Unit 1
Richmond Hill, Ontario L4B 0A7

Translator: Ivanka Hahnenberger

Printed in China

Florent Silloray

ROBERT CAPA
A Graphic Biography

FIREFLY BOOKS

"If your photographs aren't good enough, you're not close enough."

Robert Capa

Klosters, Swiss Alps, January 1954.

This damn backache just won't let up...

I haven't slept well in weeks.

I'm tired.

Really tired.

And it's wearing me down.

Forcing myself to rest does nothing.

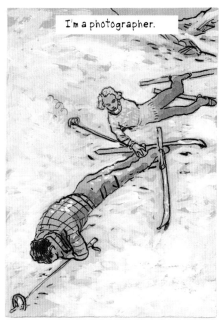

I'm a photographer.

Lately, I've been making the rounds at upmarket resorts for the American magazine *Holiday*.

When I'm not doing that, I run the Paris office of the Magnum Photos Agency, which I co-founded in 1947.

I'm considered by many as the greatest war photographer in the world.

But I quit the battlefields in 1945.

I even refused to cover the Korean War for *LIFE* magazine, my high-profile client.

I was born Endre Friedmann in Budapest in 1913, but I am known by my alias.

Robert Capa.

This is my last winter...

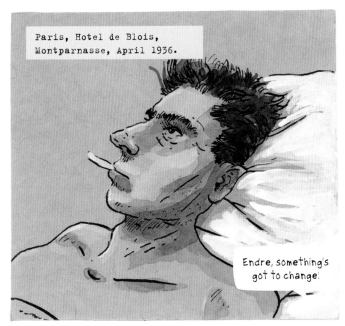

Paris, Hotel de Blois, Montparnasse, April 1936.

Endre, something's got to change!

Yesterday, I managed to sell two of your photos to the Alliance agency.

Well done!

I got a letter from Buda, Gerda. Mom promised that, in her next package, she'll send me some shoes and some stockings and a corset from her boutique for you.

Endre, I am not spending another summer in this damp room.

We have to start making some money.

I have had my shoes resoled five times now.

I may have an idea.

Ready for your only meal of the day?

Two large coffees with cream and two day-old croissants, please.

You could pretend to be a mysterious and talented foreign photographer...

...a rich American.

I would be your agent and contact newspapers and agencies.

You're a bit of a rogue and always on the road. So it's hard to pin you down.

With that cover story, we could increase your rates.

Hey, there's Chim and Cartier-Bresson.

Gerda wants me to pretend to be an American.

Now, we just need a name.

John...

Morris...

Robert...

Robert... Robert Capa.

Paris, Café le Dome, June 1936.
Dear Mom,...

...Big changes are happening here...

...Gerda had a fantastic idea...

...goodbye, chronic poverty...

...she has made it so we can sell my photos at 500 francs each...

...I have even been hired by a big leftist newspaper, Vu...

...I have been asked to cover the summer of the Popular Front...

...our little white lie is working...

...and my photos are a huge hit...

...Lucien Vogel, the editor in chief of the journal, figured it out, though...

...I was called into his office to explain myself...

...our little tale made him laugh, but that ended Gerda's high prices...

...we have lost some income, true, but I now have a bond with Vogel...

...Your son, Endre.

Paris, Café le Dome, July 1936.

First Hungary, Germany and Italy ...now fascism is rising in Spain. Endre, I hope that France will stand up for the young Spanish Republic.

Photos of the events are missing from this article on the war down there.

You're wanted on the phone, Mr. Capa.

Hello, Capa, it's Vogel. I am sending you and Gerda to Barcelona on the next train.

...capture the sentiments of combat ...sure, OK.

It's an excellent opportunity for you to learn by doing. You know everything you need to about the camera.

We'll see.

Barcelona, Estació de França, August 1936.

We arrived in a city buzzing feverishly.

You couldn't miss the armed movements and political activists on every street corner.

And those thousands of smiles I captured on film.

MILICIES OBRERES
OFICINA D'ALLISTME

POUM
POUM

The infectious joy of this populist fervor.

Barcelona was just one big republican demonstration, where a hundred thousand chests offered themselves to the bullets of the fascists at the Southern Front.

Tanned, wiry men holding their rifles aloft.

Groups of children jumping out of the way of the column of trucks squeaking under the weight of the arms they bore.

Daily newspapers draped over old crates interspersed among the crowds on terraces under the burning sun.

The Front in Cordoba, September 1936.

Huesca, Toledo, it had been two months, with no sign of celebration of a victory over Franco's tyranny.

The republicans were retreating on all fronts.

Gerda and I worked like a well-oiled machine.

We ran from one trench to another, getting as close as possible to our fighting comrades.

Her shadow, always a few inches away allowed me to defy the odds of flying shrapnel.

I had to live up to the reputation that she invented of Capa.

La pequeña rubia... ...the little blond.

I could sense the men looking at her.

Her images were filled with her charm and talent, and her contact sheets confirmed it.

She was improving quickly, and we used to tussle for the best angle, which she had a real eye for.

We'd send our negatives off together to Paris. Sometimes her photos were credited to Capa.

That infuriated her.

On the road, retreating to Madrid, September 1936.

Gerda, when we get to Madrid, let's get married.

Hey, Capa, can you really see me, Gerda Taro, subjugating myself to the bourgeois institution of marriage?

How could you even think of it here in full flight? Amongst thousands of corpses and with hordes of wounded and orphans everywhere.

Our negatives are oozing death, Capa.

I only want one thing: victory.

Courageous republicans avenge the strings of bombs from Guernica to Madrid.

A headline with our photos in the announcements that our friends at the Dome would see in *Ce Soir*.

Never bring it up again.

...ever.

February 1937, second trip to Madrid.

We made a quick round-trip to Paris.

Visiting the journals that were publishing our photos. The editor in chief of *Ce Soir* was wildy enthusiastic.

We sold our photos to *Regards*, *Paris Soir* and some British, Russian, Catalonian and Hungarian papers.

I was told that I had found my style. A series of photos at the heart of the action with short, well-thought-out captions. The editors ate it up.

Gerda's courage impressed me more and more each day.

The air raid sirens didn't even make her blink.

We made our headquarters the Hotel Florida.

It was the Madrid hangout for foreign correspondents.

Ernest Hemingway — who was there covering the war for several American papers — and I tried to drink the bar dry every day.

Well, Capa, everyone's talking about you.

CAPA!

Your photos are on every page.

And once again, I am not credited for this photo!

But, Gerda, my name is not mentioned more than yours is.

That's not an excuse. It really bugs those bastards that a female photographer is dodging bullets.

Capa, your wife's something.

She's not my wife...

Marry her quick, before she gets away.

As soon as the sirens go off, I grab my camera bag and head for the closest trolley stop.

The front, in the capital, moved every day. The war in Madrid had the peculiarity that we could get there by trolley, you just had to be careful where you got off so that you didn't find yourself on the wrong side.

The constant shelling was terrifying.

There was a fierce battle around the Parque del Buen Retiro.

My jacket was stained with blood and my camera out of film. I jumped on the trolley and headed back to the Hotel Florida.

It was surreal: people were killing each other less than a kilometer away, and we were here consuming world-class wines and pastries.

With Gerda the mood was explosive.

I have to go back to Paris for a few weeks.

Aragon, the head of *Ce Soir* has asked me to.

That time I went back alone. Gerda insisted on staying. She screamed it like a prayer. "A republican victory is in sight! It's imminent!"

And she wanted to cover the second writer's conference that was going to take place in Madrid.

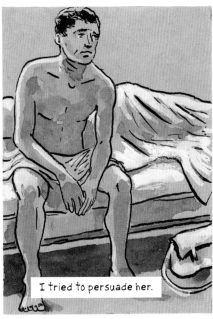

I tried to persuade her.

Nothing worked.

I left her in the care of the wonderful Ted Allen, a Canadian comrade who was a political commissioner to a medical unit.

I left Madrid in the beginning of July 1937.

I tried until the day I left.

Things happened fast in Paris. I was made *Ce Soir*'s official photographer.

I took advantage of my new position to promote Chim and Cartier-Bresson.

We were now all working for a salary and free to choose our subjects.

We finally got what we wanted: financial and editorial independence.

I founded the Robert Capa Studio in my new apartment on rue Froidevaux.

It was my compatriot and friend Csiki Weisz who developed the negatives, played secretary and archivist while we were away.

evacuad MADRID

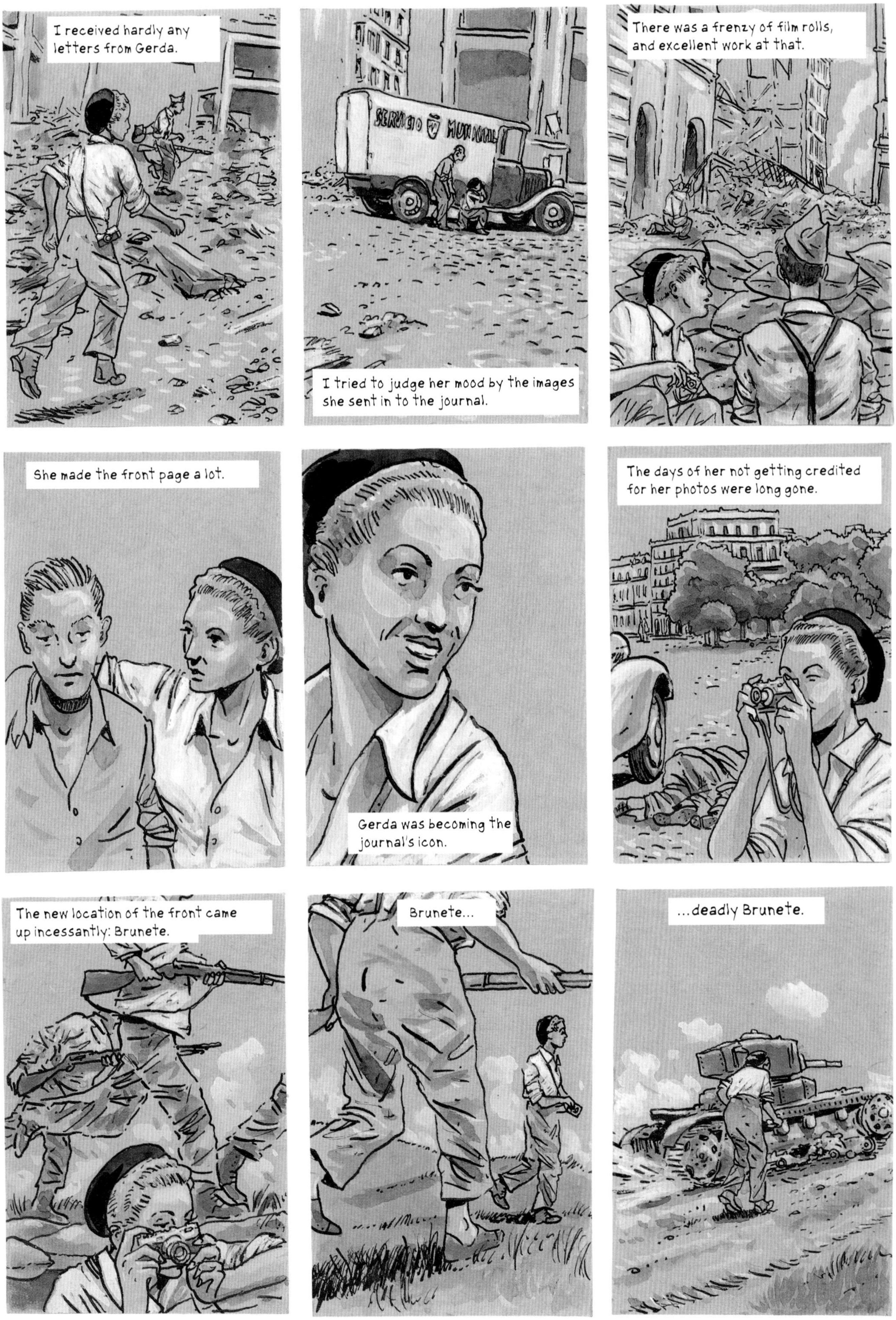

I received hardly any letters from Gerda.
SERVICIO MUNICIPAL
I tried to judge her mood by the images she sent in to the journal.
There was a frenzy of film rolls, and excellent work at that.
She made the front page a lot.
Gerda was becoming the journal's icon.
The days of her not getting credited for her photos were long gone.
The new location of the front came up incessantly: Brunete.
Brunete...
...deadly Brunete.

End of July 1937, Paris.
Terrace of the Dome.

Hello ... *Ce Soir?*

It's Capa ... May I speak to the editor in chief?

Yes, I'm really sorry. I tried to reach you... Yes... it's been confirmed.

Her body will be repatriated to Paris on the next train.

Nothing to be done...

She got caught in the treads of a tank in Brunete...

...a republican tank.

Paris, July 30, 1937.

Gerda's death made the front page of *l'Humanité*. She was the first female photographer to be killed in action.

She was elevated to the level of saint of the antifascist cause. Even *LIFE* magazine did an article on her.

Thousands of Parisians accompanied the procession all the way to Père-Lachaise.

Her brothers were furious at me for having taught her how to use a Leica.

I was told that, as she was dying, she asked about her cameras.

She was going to be turning 27.

I had abandoned her in the danger.

She would still be alive if I'd stayed with her in Spain.

I would not have let her stand on the footboard of the car that was run over by the tank.

I'd have stopped her.

Taken her place.

Gerda Taro... born Gerta Pohorylle.

Gerda... "*pequeña rubia,*" that lovely name they gave her down there...

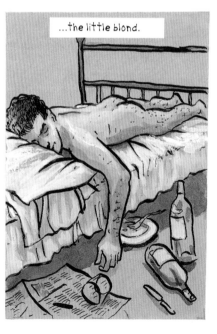

...the little blond.

Gerda... my love.

26

Marseille, January 21, 1938.

Joris Ivens, a filmmaker friend who I met at the front in Spain, decided to put me back in the saddle. I was off to China, where the Japanese had invaded.

I was dubbed assistant director of the film we were going to shoot there. *LIFE* wanted some photos of the battles, as well.

With John Fernhout, the project's official cameraman, and other Spanish War companions, I set off to join Ivens in Hong Kong.

Ivens didn't hide the fact that it was to be a propaganda film to glorify the alliance that the nationalists and the communists formed against imperialist Japan.

The 26 days at sea were filled with the inflexible ship-board protocol.

Apparently, we were disturbing the ladies in second class. We laughed too loudly and our antics were in poor taste.

Fernhout gave it his all, trying to get me to forget my Paris demons.

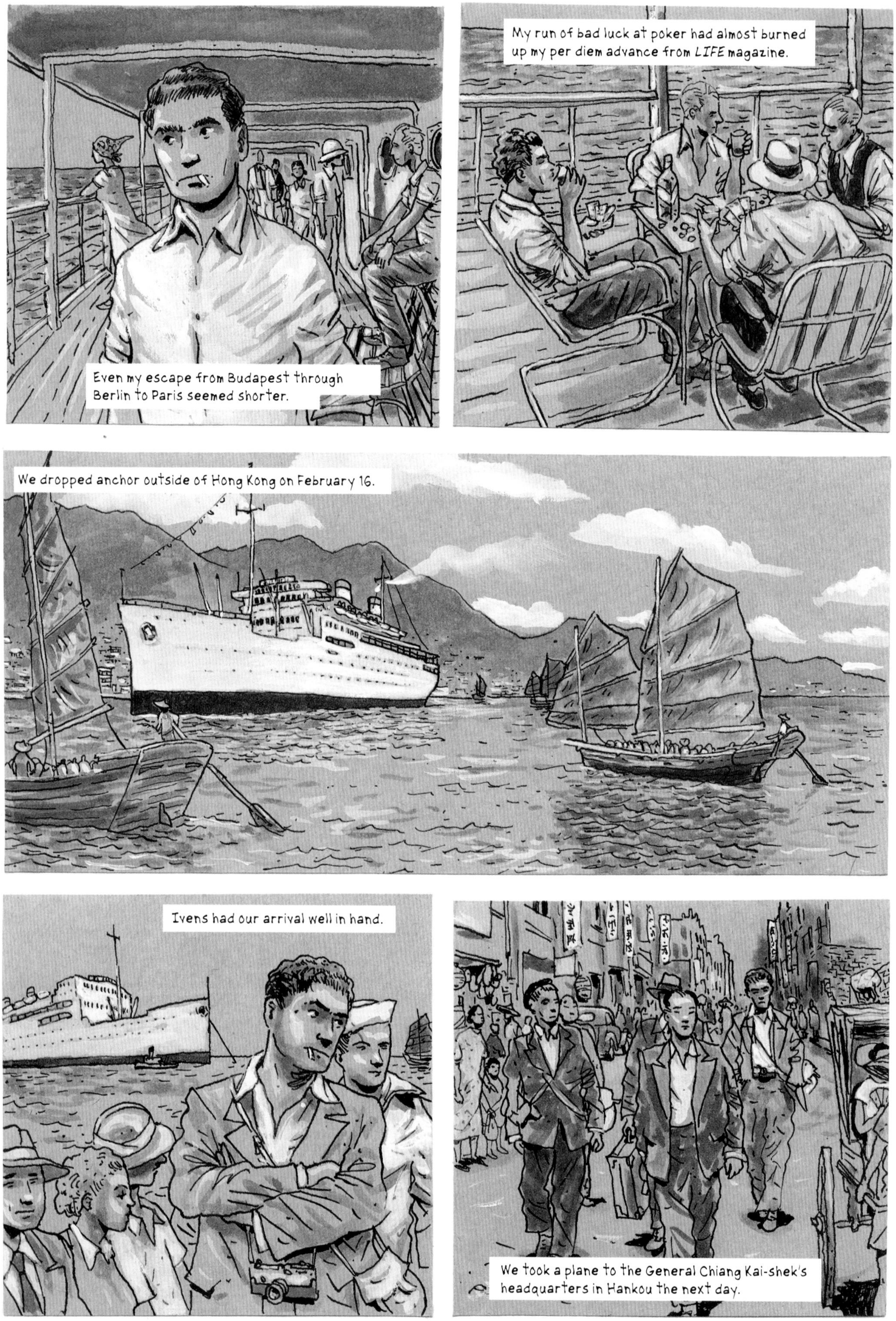
Even my escape from Budapest through Berlin to Paris seemed shorter.
My run of bad luck at poker had almost burned up my per diem advance from *LIFE* magazine.
We dropped anchor outside of Hong Kong on February 16.
Ivens had our arrival well in hand.
We took a plane to the General Chiang Kai-shek's headquarters in Hankou the next day.

We were constantly surrounded by nationalist chaperones. We quickly realized that our cowboy methods would not be accepted here.

We soon met Mrs. Chiang Kai-shek.

She was a personal friend of the big boss of *LIFE*, Henry Luce.

She was quite interested in me, being a photographer on contract for *LIFE*.

Our repeated requests to go to the front were diplomatically ignored.

Pointless to hope to film the communists. For Mrs. Chiang Kai-Shek the nationalists were only defending the country.

We played the parts of complacent reporters so as to win over our hosts.

We were taken around the garrisons farthest from the front.

The *Picture Post* may have considered me the greatest war photographer in the world, but Ivens could not have cared less, and confined me to the lowly position of second cameraman.

The militaristic management of the crew...

...and constantly being ordered around by the director were weighing on me.

I did sometimes break away from the group with my Leica to immerse myself in local village life.

At the beginning of April, we were finally sent to the front in the northeast in Suzhou. The incessant Japanese shelling during the train ride was unbearable.

Mrs. Chiang Kai-shek's chaperones complicated our shoot.

We entered Taierzhuang, a town taken back from the Japanese just days after the first Chinese victory.

My photos were published in the May 23, 1938, issue of *LIFE*. The magazine article stated that I had been there for the big battle, when in fact the Nationalist Army officers blocked our access to the front. At the heat of the battle, I was snoring in my tent.

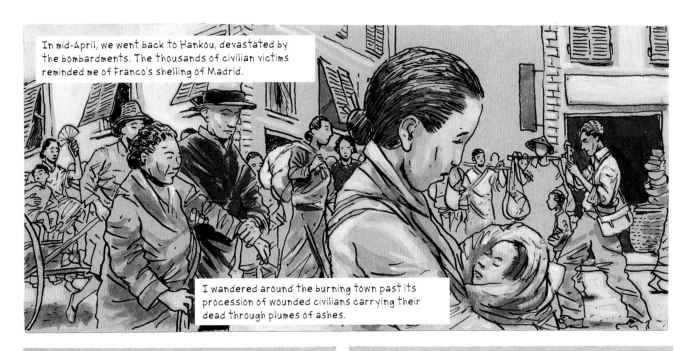

In mid-April, we went back to Hankou, devastated by the bombardments. The thousands of civilian victims reminded me of Franco's shelling of Madrid.

I wandered around the burning town past its procession of wounded civilians carrying their dead through plumes of ashes.

By dragging me to China, Joris Ivens wanted to get me out of my Paris lethargy, but this place brought back all of the horrors of Spain and Gerda's death.

In the beginning of August, he went back to New York with Fernhout, to edit the film, leaving me alone in that hell.

I tried to drown the editorial staff of LIFE magazine in photos. I was taking my first color shots with Kodak 35 mm film.

I couldn't wait to see them printed.

The Japanese were a few miles away. I didn't want to witness this new fascist victory. I felt like a scavenger feeding the newspapers with a regular daily dose of dead bodies. I went back to Europe.

Spain, October 25, 1938.

Hankou had fallen to the Japanese.

The Munich agreements were signed on September 30. Europe bowed to Hitler.

Stalin had just ordered the Russian volunteers in Spain to abandon the republic.

I covered the last march of the international brigades down the Diagonale in Barcelona.

I'd spent seven years in Europe running from the fascists. The Spanish Republic was going to die, and I was walking with the funeral procession.

Seeing my comrades on the way to defeat, I had to push my tears back behind my viewfinder and grit my teeth.

What purpose had all the risks and photos we took at the sides of the fighters served...?

...and Gerda's death?

This life as an itinerant photographer, does it make any sense?

Being dependent on newspaper editors without having any control of the work?

On the plane on the way back from China, an idea came to me.

A revolutionary idea.

Start an agency cooperative for young, independent, talented photographers.

We'd keep the rights to our images, no longer giving them to the newspapers. And we would no longer be employees.

We could negotiate our own rates and bank the rights fees that we invoiced at each use.

I talked to Chim Seymour, Cartier-Bresson and others. They were all on board, but a few of them said that the papers would never go for it.

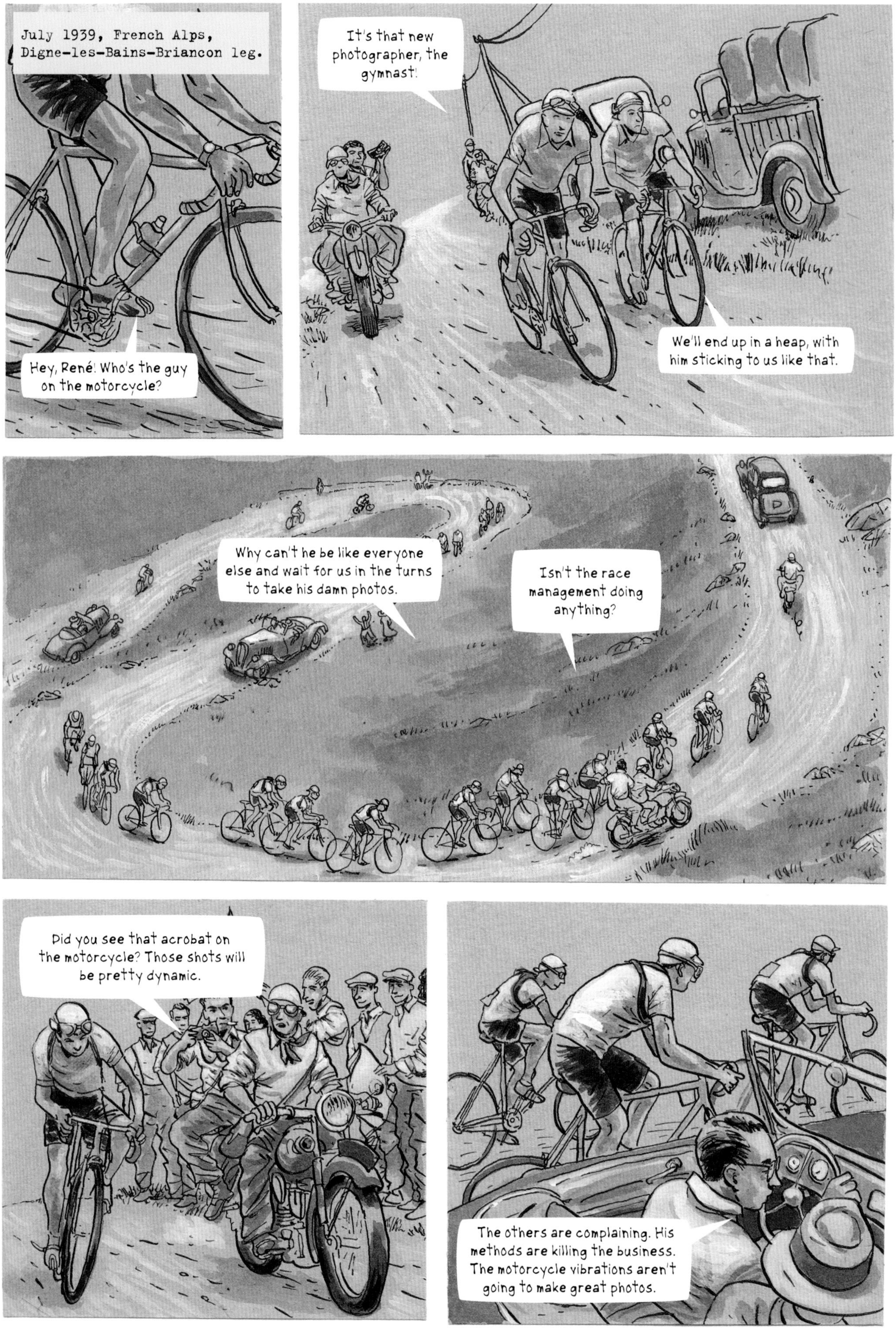
July 1939, French Alps,
Digne-les-Bains-Briancon leg.
Hey, René! Who's the guy on the motorcycle?
It's that new photographer, the gymnast!
We'll end up in a heap, with him sticking to us like that.
Why can't he be like everyone else and wait for us in the turns to take his damn photos.
Isn't the race management doing anything?
Did you see that acrobat on the motorcycle? Those shots will be pretty dynamic.
The others are complaining. His methods are killing the business. The motorcycle vibrations aren't going to make great photos.

Paris Match asked me to cover the Tour de France.

The motorcycle was part of the deal.

I asked my friend Taci to drive me around for a month.

Apparently, that was not done: taking pictures of the racers at full speed from the back of a motorcycle.

The editorial staff of *Paris Match* complained about my lack of interest in the drama of the race.

Apparently, I spent too much time on the side of the road, shooting the spectators in the villages.

Paris, 37 rue Froidevaux, Capa Studio, September 1939.

Yes, this is Danton 75-21... a call from the Chilean consulate...? Yes, I accept.

Well, hello, comrade... So, the visa?

I've been waiting for weeks; you're my last hope.

I need to get to my family in New York...

You're a lifesaver, Pablo. I'll stop by the consulate this afternoon.

That was Pablo Neruda at the Chilean Consulate. He's a poet I met in Spain during the Civil War. He has an important position and was able to get me a visa, which I needed in order to leave for America right away.

36

Solidarity amongst Spanish republicans.

My ship, *The Manhattan*, is leaving from Le Havre in three days.

Csiki, I have to leave the archives behind.

My friend, I am counting on you to take care of them.

Chim left me his negatives. And even more valuable...

I want you to take care of Gerda's, as well.

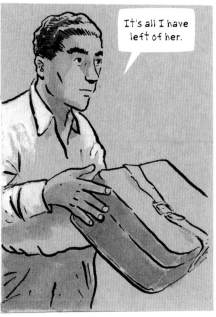

It's all I have left of her.

If the Nazis reach Paris, find a safe hiding place.

Keep an eye on her relics.

I'm counting on you.

37

On board the SS *Manhattan*, Port of New York, October 1939.

Finally, I would see my family again...

...in a country where I would have to start all over.

Since 1937, my mother, Julia, and my brother, Cornell, lived in a run-down apartment on West 94th street.

My mother's goulash didn't always make up for the weight of being back in a family setting.

It was like being back in the apartment in Buda in the 20s, the clutter, the fits, the arguments...

The traces of the family tailor shop, sold during the Great Depression, invaded my room — clients trying on half-tailored suits in the hall or the living room. This hive-like existence made me dream of faraway places.

The high cost of living in New York forced me to get back at it.

I had thought, with fame and honors from Spain and China, that I'd get a warmer welcome than I did from the editor at *LIFE*.

When Edward Thomson, the editor-in-chief, heard my English, he cringed and gave me a few pitiful assignments.

Settling into the nightlife was easier. New York revealed itself as being full of beautiful women, ready to be charmed.

I stretched the evenings out as long as possible, avoiding going home to my room crisscrossed with clotheslines.

Through my friends from the magazine and the Photo Pix agency, I tried to improve my syntax and my aces-high.

Julia moaned and complained, but my status as favorite son allowed me to avoid a lot of arguments.

LIFE sent me out West to New Mexico, to capture the souls of cowboys and celebrities whose names I can't remember.

I was happy to be assigned a photo shoot of my old friend Hemingway and his family for the December 1939 issue.

For several nights in a row, we relived our Spanish Civil War days, and my father's high-end whiskey made me forget the good Burgundies that were missing this side of the Atlantic.

Then it was sin city, Calumet City, where the saloons were filled with alcoholic workers.

The LIFE subjects were too ordinary and predictable. Henry Luce's periodical was like a giant advertising rag on luxury paper that sold 3 million copies a week.

I was far from my Paris communist papers and my freedom to travel.

In early 1940 I got an expiry notice from the department of immigration. My visa was running out.

My Hungarian stateless passport prevented me from extending it. It was time for a quick solution.

I needed to marry an American.

Through mutual friends I met Toni Sorel, a magnificent brunette. A freelance model taking dance classes.

With two German refugee photographer friends, Otto Hagel and Hansel Mieth, we arranged a small matrimonial road trip to Maryland, land of the quick weddings.

Toni and I made a deal. In exchange for a marriage of convenience, I agreed to pay for my future wife's dance classes.

A bribe to a crooked doctor allowed us to have certificates stating that my fiancée was pregnant.

After our moment with the justice of the peace, we went and celebrated right away, before we reconsidered, especially since the little certificates had set us back significantly.

Toni did not appreciate my wandering hands on the trip back. That was not part of the arrangement.

There were tears when we dropped her off at the Lincoln Tunnel. I headed uptown, to the Bedford Hotel.

The U.S. government required that I leave the country for six months before I could come back and stay legally.

LIFE made me an offer I couldn't refuse to cover the upcoming Mexican presidential election.

I was told to expect a rather violent environment and some pretty intense local political customs.

The generous advance allowed me to settle into the Hotel Montejo, second-rate palace and den of confirmed European spies, and incidentally, the employer of the country's best bartender.

Opposing sides were clashing. On the one side, General Manuel Ávila Camacho, hero of the left; on the other, General Juan Almazán, champion of the authoritarian conservative camp.

The Nazi agents did all they could to prejudice the general consensus against the Franco-English-American alliance.

At every demonstration, several people were shot as the crowd dispersed.

It was all about insurrection, and it felt a bit like I was back in the fervor of Barcelona in the summer of '37, but with sombreros and cactuses this time.

I spent most of my time at the Montejo.

It was a den of thieves, where the Nazi agents were trying to destabilize a U.S. border country. The old Spanish republicans were everywhere, as were Stalin's spies.

The posh clients complained to the management about our behavior.

For a few days, we kept coming across a dark, silent man, who seemed to be pretty nervous. He called himself Frank Jackson. His real name was Ramon Mercader, and he was one of Stalin's men.

We learned that on the night before, that of August 20, 1940, he'd put a bullet in Trotsky's head while he was hiding out in Coyoacan, a suburb of Mexico City.

I got there too late. The police had already closed off access to the house. It was impossible to take photos of the scene of the crime.

It reminded me of my first scoop. In 1932, in Copenhagen...

...during one of his speeches, I managed to trick the paranoid Trotsky and take pictures of him from just below the stage he was on. This series of out-of-focus shots was one of my first great feats.

Trotsky was taken to the hospital, but died after several agonizing hours.

I sneaked into the cremation. The door to the oven didn't close properly. Everyone was mesmerized watching the revolutionary go up in flames.

Border crossing, Laredo Texas, October 10, 1940.

The six months had passed. I could finally go back to the U.S.

With my shiny new visa, I went back to New York, the magazine and the family apartment.

LIFE sent me off to Sun Valley, Idaho.

It was for a long feature on the most famous writer of the time, my old friend Ernest Hemingway.

Eight pages, including several color photos to honor the literary giant at the peak of his fame. The magazine was counting on our friendship resulting in very up-front and personal photos.

Papa Hemingway had just sold the rights to *For Whom the Bell Tolls* to Hollywood for a record sum of $150,000. Gary Cooper, who was to play the lead, spent a few hours with us.

Hemingway was dead set on getting me a bit part in the film, which was how I got wrapped up in a series of long, alcohol-fueled evenings with Hollywood players.

I tried to capture the fragile environment of his office. I had a lot of trouble convincing his third wife, Martha, to take part.

I couldn't deny it, I missed Europe. France's defeat and Paris' being occupied and draped in swastikas sickened me.

I wondered about the studio on rue Froidevaux and my friends stuck in France. My work was empty. Meaningless assignments. Europe was the place to be — in England, where the English were still resisting Hitler's bombings.

That day, I received two letters. One was from the Department of Justice, saying that since I was Hungarian one of the access powers and thus an enemy state, I had to turn in all my cameras, binoculars and weapons. Any trips farther than 10 miles needed to be authorized.

The other was from Collier's magazine, offering me an assignment in England. A check for an advance of $1,500 was also in the envelope. I had 48 hours to find transportation.

FINAL MORNING EXTRA
BLITZ ON LONDON
WAR!

March, 1942, onboard a naval convoy.

Since Pearl Harbor, America was at war. It was my second time crossing the Atlantic. I was finally on my way to London, to cover the war.

This time, aboard a Norwegian cargo vessel chartered by Cunard Lines that was taking military personnel to England. The rear admiral, an old, gray-haired sea dog, who was the commander of the convoy, confused me with Frank Capra.

I did nothing to dispel the misconception because, thanks to the rear admiral's position, doors opened, allowing me to shoot an anthology of the crossing. In exchange, I had to spend dinners at the captain's table, making up Hollywood anecdotes.

The 44 vessels dodged through the foggy hunting ground of the German submarines.

To forget the fear that filled the vessel, I tested a new Contax II with a roll of Kodachrome. I even had access to the radio room, whose windows were awash with seawater and from which I watched our jerky advance, not actually abating the fear.

The Irish admiral's admiration for the silent film stars forced me to repeat my recent lies about Lillian Gish or Gloria Swanson. I pulled my inspiration as an imposter from my flask of bourbon.

The first time we played hide-and-seek with Nazi submarines in the middle of the Atlantic, I prayed to my guardian angels to get me to England safe and sound.

The crew had some big poker players. My little nest egg got smaller as we pushed forward toward England.

The rear admiral, in an attempt to lure the U-boats, decided to bury us in an extremely photogenic smoky fog. I shot with color and black-and-white film, leaving it up to the editors to decide which was best.

Border control gave me a hard time. My status as war photographer, and permanent American resident of Hungarian origin was complicating my getting in.

It was thanks to the Hungarian origins of the commander of the port of Belfast's wife that I was allowed to disembark onto British soil...

...and be invited to dinner at their home. They even organized a special plane the next day to fly me to London, where I then settled into the Savoy.

The nicest suite in the place was where Quentin Reynold and his Collier'steam had their London headquarters. Reynolds recommended me to the U.S. Army press office.

I had to go through the Military Intelligence, the only people authorized to issue me a long-term press pass. The pretty redhead who handled my case succumbed to the Hungarian charm, and I thanked her for the precious document by inviting her to dinner that same evening.

The _Illustrated_, an English weekly, offered me 100 pounds for reprints of my Collier's photo essays. This helped me cover my losses at the poker table.

I stopped by to see my Spanish Civil War friends, now colleagues at the London LIFE bureau. They agreed to develop the film from the Atlantic convoy crossing. A friend of mine who worked as an editorial secretary typed and corrected my article so I could submit it to the censors.

I slid myself into the daily life of Londoners that was being tried by daily bombings.

Some families even invited me to share meals with them. I was often sent home heavier with vegetables, bread and cheese that supplemented my daily rations.

With the hems of my trousers red with brick dust, I was reminded of climbing through ruins in Spain and China.

August 1941.
Chelveston Air Base.

The Illustrated got me an invitation to visit the 301st bomber group of the USAF based north of London.

I got a very warm welcome from the kids who were piloting those flying fortresses.

With a bottle of warm beer in hand, I jumped into a diabolical game of cards. An airman's version of poker.

My amateur antics and abilities made me the brunt of much laughter.

I was allowed to attend the mission briefing, but low cloud cover kept the planes grounded.

The pilots went back to their poker games, journals and warm beers.

The weather kept the planes on the ground for four days. I had all the time in the world to take pictures of my hosts and their shiny B-17s.

The morning of the fifth day, the siren for takeoff ripped through the air, and I followed my poker companions to their planes.

When the last B-17 disappeared into the clouds, I checked my watch.

Six hours to wait in front of silent radios before the first of the boys would be back.

Of the 24 planes that had left that morning, a squadron of only 17 planes returned to Chelveston Air Base.

One of the first planes back came in on its belly. I used up the whole roll in my first Contax.

The firefighting foam getting shot out of the truck's cannon in color: bingo! The machine-gun pilot being evacuated by the medics: snap, snap! The plane's propellers deformed by the fuselage scraping the ground: a great catch.

One of my new poker pals climbed out of the cockpit, bloody. He let me have it.

Are these the pictures you were hoping for, photographer?!

Ashamed of myself, I put away my Contax and headed for the first train back to London.

I didn't want to be one of those vultures who took photos of the consequences of the war without seeing the action.

My editors loved my dramatic photo-essays of the 301 squadron. But I wanted to feel the breath of combat...

...and the adrenaline of the front that I'd discovered in Spain.

One morning, the head of *Illustrated* and a high-ranking officer from the Army Press Office came to my room at the Savoy with the daily paper under their arm.

Did you take this picture?

Do you realize what you've taken?

Yes, a great cover photo, sir.

Don't be a wise ass, Capa!

Do you see that small black dot on the front glass of the B-17? That is the new Norden bombsight.

A new top secret military element, and you've put it on the front page.

But my photos have all gone through the censors.

If you were enlisted, you'd be court-martialed for this, Capa.

We're going to have to destroy 400,00 copies.

You are confined to your hotel until further notice.

51

The next day I was called to my first hearing. I defended myself to some stern officers in my bad English mixed with Hungarian.

As witness for the defense, the pilot whose photo I had taken, Lieutenant Bishop, was more convincing. The decorated war hero managed to get me off with a warning and a new position.

I celebrated by getting myself a hand-tailored uniform on Savile Row.

While waiting for my next mission, one to North Africa, I went to visit some old friends, refugees, where I had a long-standing invitation.

A friend of the family was monopolizing the gramophone.

Her blond, almost venetian pink, hair did not excuse her from her passion for Tino Rossi and kept distracting me from my reading.

After dinner, she got it in her head to teach me how to rumba.

After a couple of grimaces from feeling my two left feet, she whispered her name: Elaine.
                    I call her Pinky.

The concierge at the Savoy called to let me know everyone was looking for me. My ship was to sail from Glasgow in 48 hours.

Pinky dropped me off at the closest railway station, mumbling in French, "I'll wait for you..."

Spring 1943, near Gibraltar.

We were heading at a good clip toward the Algerian coast, a bit behind the main body of the fleet that had launched Operation Torch.

Planned simultaneous landings in Algeria and Morocco to set up the head of the allied force against the Afrika Corps.

Since the victories at El Alamein and Stalingrad, the winds seemed to have changed.

I, along with the fresh Scottish troops that my vessel carried, came ashore in Algiers at the beginning of March.

When I got there, I was told that the front was holding at a couple hundred kilometers from the Tunisian border.

I was assigned a Jeep and a driver who brought me to the fighting by dodging the smoking bodies abandoned by the Axis powers.

The roads linking the rare villages were mined. The furrowed brows of my guardian angel dissuaded me from playing tourist.

The blinding white light reminded me of the hills of Andalucía.

We caught up to General Patton's brigade in an oasis near Gafsa.

He let me trail him so I could take pictures. I remember the Colt .45 with the ivory crosses that hung from his hip.

Far from the frustration of the English airfields, I found the excitement I'd discovered in Spain.

My camera just kept clicking. I kept on immortalizing the soldiers' fun-loving faces.

In the palm groves of El Guettar, the soldiers perched on their war booty were not camera shy.

The officers allowed me to get really close to the fighting.

Our crest line was subject to heavy shelling for three days by Rommel's troops, now at bay.

The dust from the first line of German prisoners of war covered my 50 mm lens as I took their picture.

At nightfall, after we had had our rations, I quickly wrote down the photos I'd taken for bylines before I joined the others for some poker.

Kairouan, North Africa, base of the 82nd paratrooper's division. July 1943.

I received a cable from Collier's. My credentials and my contract had expired. I was ordered back to New York.

Desperate to stay on the front with the victory that seemed inevitable, I decided to press my luck.

I stepped in for a fellow photographer who was supposed to jump into Sicily with the 82nd Airborne under the orders of General Ridgway. I manage to meet the general, and knowing my work, he authorizes me to go along.

I did not tell him about my expired credentials.

If I was caught I'd be court-martialed.

I quickly made an offer to LIFE magazine.

I'm not allowed to jump with the first wave.

I entered Sicily by the small southern port of Licata.

I followed behind the 1st Division that was on the heels of the collapsing German army and their backup Italian troops.

I learned from the commanding officers that I am the only photographer who is witnessing the beginning of the liberation of Europe. And without valid credentials!

The Sicilians were very welcoming. My dark skin and mop of dark hair made me look like a local. That was the best passport I could have had for using my Leica and getting some wine for my escorts.

After the harsh battle at Troina, I run into General Teddy Roosevelt, who congratulated me on my new assignment. I had just become the official correspondent for LIFE magazine.

Outside of Naples, September 1943.

The battles for the liberation of Naples were the fiercest I had ever witnessed.

I spent several days under the shelling of German howitzers on a farm in the mountains that the Rangers had turned into a type of fort and nicknamed Fort Schuster.

The things I witnessed in the streets of Naples broke my heart.

Piles of bodies filled the streets.

It was as though the Nazis were punishing Italy for their defeat.

I went into a photographing frenzy.

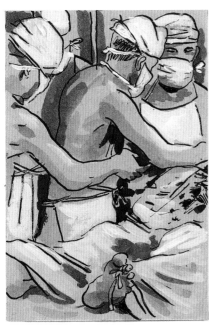

I had to get this mass of cadavers into my darkroom.

I had to...

The Normandy Coast, June 6, 1944.

I do not know by what miracle I got out of the battle for Italy alive. Hand-to-hand combat on Monte Cassino; my rolls of film covered in blood, rusted by the rocks of Abruzzo.

I arrived in London at the beginning of April 1944, having left my two colleagues Slim Aarons and Ernie Pyle behind, wounded by a bomb at Anzio.

The invasion of France was being prepared, and I put in my dibs.

There were several photographers who had credentials for D-day.

I put everything on the 2nd Battalion of the 116th Infantry that was to debark in the first wave of the assault on Omaha beach, sector Easy Red.

The few nights that I spent in the arms of Pinky did not manage to calm the visions that haunted my insomnia.

The officers from the press office asked two things of me...

...to write down my last wishes and my blood type.

My regulation Hamilton watch showed that the gate dropped down just after 6:30.

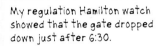

I had two Contax with me. One was army issue. They were both sealed in a bag along with my unexposed film.

I dodged the pools of vomit and shit that cover the bottom of the barge.

Deafened by the shelling raining down on us, the sounds of masses of machine-gun fire in the distance were almost cancelled out.

It's all guesswork; my hands were shaking uncontrollably. **CLICK.**

I clutched my camera. **CLICK.**

You are not really here. **CLICK.**

Glue your eye to the viewfinder. Kurva!*

That isn't the guy who was just throwing up a moment ago, whose guts are bouncing in the waves. **CLICK.**

*A Hungarian curse word meaning "whore."

59

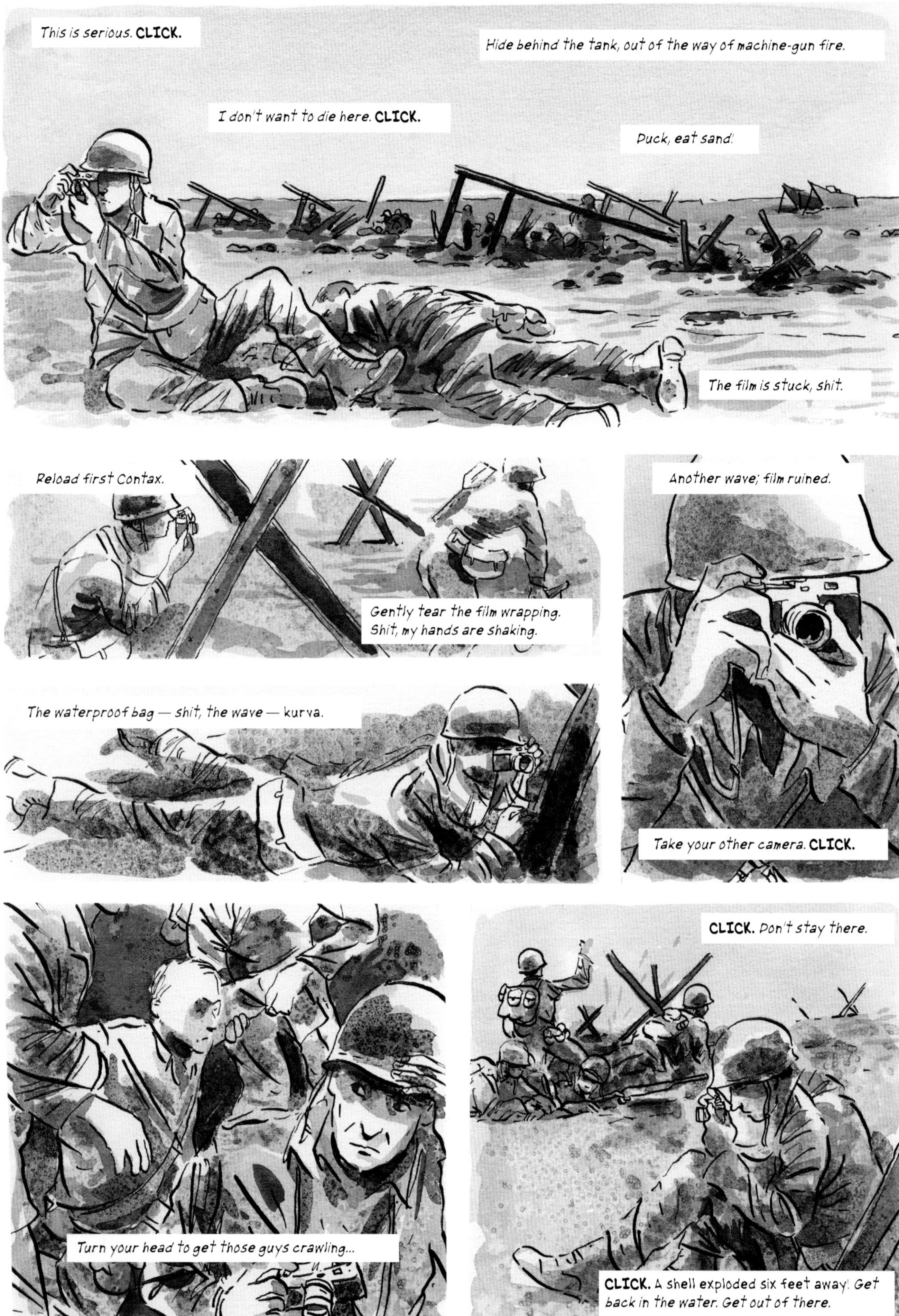
This is serious. **CLICK.**
Hide behind the tank, out of the way of machine-gun fire.
I don't want to die here. **CLICK.**
Duck, eat sand!
The film is stuck, shit.
Reload first Contax.
Gently tear the film wrapping. Shit, my hands are shaking.
Another wave; film ruined.
Take your other camera. **CLICK.**
The waterproof bag — shit, the wave — kurva.
Turn your head to get those guys crawling...
CLICK. Don't stay there.
CLICK. A shell exploded six feet away! Get back in the water. Get out of there.

Hold the waterproof bag close.

Protect your cameras, dipshit.

KURVA! *The barge is less than 150 feet away.*

Kurva, *the bodies rolling in the waves are preventing you from advancing.*

The water is wild, kurva. The water is freezing.

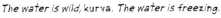

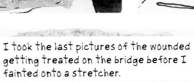

Kurva!

With an LCI(L)-94, I got back to the Samuel Chase. As soon as I got on board, my shaking was replaced by exhaustion.

I took the last pictures of the wounded getting treated on the bridge before I fainted onto a stretcher.

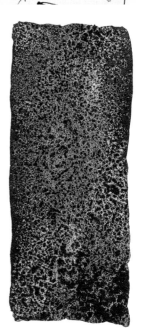

London, *LIFE* bureau, morning of June 7, 1944.

Where is Capa? The photos need to be at the New York office by June 10 at the latest!

He called from Weymouth. They just landed, and his film is arriving by air courier.

The others only brought in photos that are unusable or they didn't even debark. I need photos for the *LIFE* D-day special. For Pete's sake.

A few hours later, John Morris, *LIFE's* London photo editor, was holding my first Omaha contact sheets in his hands.

They're all grainy and shaky!

Eleven photos is all we have, John.

My photos were rushed through the censors in the middle of the night.

A race against the clock began.

An air bridge was created from London through Scotland, Iceland, Halifax, and finally, New York.

My photos were spread across seven pages of the June 19, 1944, issue. They didn't make the cover because they were too out of focus and shaky.

A posed portrait of Eisenhower made the cover.

But my name was honored as the only photographer who participated in the first wave of the landings.

Normandy, end of June 1944.

I joined up with Papa Hemingway in the Normandy countryside. He'd put together a small company, and together we liberated a few French villages.

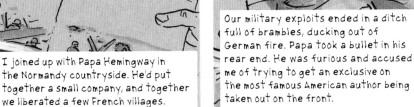

Our military exploits ended in a ditch full of brambles, ducking out of German fire. Papa took a bullet in his rear end. He was furious and accused me of trying to get an exclusive on the most famous American author being taken out on the front.

The battles in the Normandy country-side were awful. I had never seen so many dead bodies in uniform.

Chartres, August 18, 1945.

At the edge of the crowd, listening to a speech given by de Gaulle in the just-liberated town, my eye drifted to a loud group and a shaved woman by a police station.

While he spoke, General Leclerc's division was headed for Paris.

I did all I could to catch up. I wanted to be the first photographer to enter into a liberated Paris.

The night of August 24, we camped in the middle of the division.

N20 →
PARIS 6
PORTE D'ORLÉANS

Paris, August 25, 1944. Porte d'Orleans.

Leclerc's orders were that only French journalists were to enter behind his command car.

As luck would have it, I ran into two old Spanish republicans nicknamed Teruel and Brunete who were in tanks fighting in the 2nd Division. They remembered my photos from the Spanish Civil War. I was adopted as one of them, which gave me safe-conduct.

I went through my old quarter, the 14th. I could see us, Greta and I, at a table on the terrace as my Jeep passed by Le Dome.

The Parisians cheered us, and women were throwing themselves around our necks, endangering my Contax.

Paris... my Paris that I was forced to leave five years earlier.

The tears came...

The next day, I was able to infiltrate the official parade lead by de Gaulle down the Champs-Elysées.

My friend George Rodger, the photographer, had reserved a very comfortable room for me.

I was based at the Hôtel Lancaster.

Once again, I found the fervor of the 1936 demonstrations.

Isolated gunmen tried to ruin the celebrations at the Hôtel de Ville.

On June 6, 1945, in the Great Hall of the Ritz Hotel, it was love at first sight.

And the sight was Ingrid Bergman, who was on a military support tour.

She carried the aura of her newly won Oscar. She was the biggest film star of her time to have come to Paris.

With Irwin Shaw, my poker and war correspondent buddy...

...we mustered up our courage and talents to compose a note...

At exactly 6:30, magnificent, she came down the great Ritz staircase.

...with a dinner invitation for that evening.

As though it were a challenge, she said she was starving. The ice was broken.

Off to Fouquet's...

I couldn't take my eyes off her all night.

We managed to get rid of her Hollywood chaperones.

...then a champagne dinner at Maxim's.

Her beauty was unreal.

66

The summer of 1945 was cool in Paris. I took advantage of the time to visit friends.

I met up with Picasso in his studio on rue des Grands-Augustins.

He talked about the long dark age of Paris under four years of occupation.

I met up with Papa and his little band of mercenaries. We took it upon ourselves to meticulously empty all the bars of the best Paris hotels.

He was breaking up with Martha Gellhorn so he was in a terrible mood.

I gorged myself on alcohol and poker games I couldn't afford.

I learned that Pinky had married an American officer. Ingrid was off playing on army stages.

The Paris terraces were haunted by Gerda.

I got this feeling that I would never again have, in the frame of my Leica, the likes of the scenery or the soldiers of Tunisia, Monte Cassino, Omaha Beach or the jubilation of Paris.

I headed off to the front in the Ardennes, where the butchery continued through the winter of '45. I was following the American 95th Division.

Just before Christmas, I covered Patton's entry into Bastogne for *LIFE*.

I had few weeks of R&R and then followed the 17th Airborne Division, ballasted by my cameras and a bottle of whiskey in my stomach pouch.

April 1945. We were approaching Leipzig, Gerda's hometown. I wasn't going to miss the taking of that town for anything in the world.

The war was almost over. The Russians had reached Berlin, and the 2nd U.S. Infantry Division was stuck in Leipzig, near the Zeppelin bridge.

I climbed up to the top floor of a building that was still intact, with a view over the bridge. I ended up with a great photo of the last minutes of the war.

A young lieutenant mounted a machine gun on the balcony of the bourgeois apartment.

I lifted my Contax to frame my last shot of the combat, and a German sniper shot him twice.

He sank down slowly and curled up peacefully.

His fellow soldiers and I fell silent. I focused on the scarlet puddle that devoured the parquet floor. I packed up my equipment and went down to the GIs, yelling while searching for the sniper. It was my last warm cadaver of that war.

Berlin, August 1945.

We walked around the rubble that was Berlin. Ingrid is shocked by the level of destruction of this capital, where she performed in films before the war.

Berlin was unrecognizable. But I found an enthusiastic Ingrid, on tour at the front.

We even found the time to create a vignette that made her laugh uproariously: Ingrid in her bathtub.

We returned to Paris in mid--August to steal a few weeks in the whirlwind of victory.

Ingrid says she'll get a divorce so that we do not have to keep things hidden. She wants me to come to Hollywood with her.

I am now an unemployed war photographer.

I refused *LIFE*'s offer to cover the liberation of the concentration camps. I preferred to celebrate the rebirth of life and sent them an essay on the reopening of the synagogue in Berlin.

Los Angeles,
October 1945.

There were very few assignments in Europe. So, upon Ingrid's insistence, and after a few of her letters, I headed for Hollywood for a new start.

Here we had to be very careful. We no longer had the anonymity of Paris, and the tabloids could ruin my beauty's career if they found out about us.

Ingrid's credentials got me a job as a set photographer for RKO studios, which allowed me access to film shoots with the greats without any problems.

Hitchcock ended up being a wonderful accomplice, and we took refuge in the bungalows of some true friends.

I signed a writer-producer-director contract with International Pictures. I was to write my life story.

MR.HITCHCOCK   INGRID BERGM

It didn't take long to grasp the heavy administrative constraints of the system, its militarylike hierarchy, the authoritarian producers and their yes-men.

Ingrid had a hellish work schedule and was an exploited puppet of the studio, so she had little time for me.

I killed time at the sumptuous swimming pools of my new-found friends or at the poker tables of John Huston, Humphrey Bogart or Howard Hawk. We drank like fish.

70

The Santa Anita racetrack became my second office. My contract advance evaporated.

I was getting nowhere on my script. It was even torture to sit down to it.

I created a detailed guide of the bars and dives in the city of Los Angeles.

You're a slave Ingrid, a slave to your husband and the head of RKO!

We are slowly seeing less and less of each other.

You're exaggerating, Bob. It's because you're bored and you drink too much.

My dear, I saw your last film, you are really gorgeous.

You absolutely must meet my agent...

We saw them at Musso & Frank's place.

I read Slim's last script, it is incredible...

He got a $50,000 advance.

You were really at Omaha Beach...

Let's have lunch soon...

Hollywood is the biggest piece of crap I'd ever stepped in.

I discovered a different Ingrid than the one I met in Paris. She no longer took time out to live.

The studio I signed the contract with started to get uneasy as nothing came in, and they got pushy.

Ah, there you are Capa. I've been looking for you. We're shooting a scene that takes place in the early history of cinema.

Would you like to capture that on film for us?

Hitch, when does your shoot end?

End of May, if all goes well. Bob, you look awful.

I'm bored here. I feel like I'm in chains.

You have to bury yourself in work, my friend. That is rule number one in Hollywood. You don't think that I miss wonderful England? Where is your script for IP?

Getting nowhere.

I'll never get used to this town, and I miss combat action.

A photographic journalist stuck in a town and in love with an actress would make a great script, Bob!

Ingrid had finished shooting Notorious a few weeks earlier. She wanted to take a break. We packed our bags and headed off, away from the Hollywood hacks.

Jazz clubs, European films, French restaurants. I prescribed a cure of European life.

Through Italian neorealist films, I tried to prove to Ingrid that a career far from the studio formula was possible.

We even visited my mother. Ingrid took it as an omen and begged me to marry her. I explained that I was a war photographer and that peace would be broken one day.

Did she like me better free or chained down and depressed?

I'd have to pick up my cameras again and head off on an assignment for *LIFE* or some other journal, and leaving behind a wife and maybe even a child was something I couldn't do.

In August, we went back to Los Angeles because she had a new film. She, once again, convinced the director to take me on as set photographer.

I slipped into my old routine, and my drinking habits became a subject of discussion again.

Istanbul, fall 1946.

My documentary shoot was not going well. The Turkish bureaucracy ruined our stay. I am not at Ingrid's side for her triumphant premiere of Joan of Arc in New York.

I write her to tell her that I miss her terribly.

Something had snapped ...

Once my assignment was finished, I went back to New York and then we saw each other one last time in Sun Valley, in February 1947.

The last night, I lost my entire nest egg at the ski lodge casino.

I needed to find a project that paid well, and fast.

At the bar of the New York Bedford Hotel, I ran into John Steinbeck, who I'd first met in the desert during Operation Torch.

He proposed a project for a book on the USSR, illustrated by my photos. A work for four hands behind the iron curtain.

My reputation blocked me from getting a visa for the Soviet Union. I was hoping the global fame of the author of *Grapes of Wrath* would get me in.

Soviet Consulate General's office in New York, March 1947.

We are very happy to have your project, Mr. Steinbeck.

There is just one small problem.

What gave you the idea to weigh yourself down with this associate? We have many talented photographers in the Soviet Union.

That may be true ambassador, but you do not have a Robert Capa!

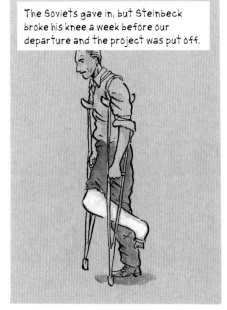

The Soviets gave in, but Steinbeck broke his knee a week before our departure and the project was put off.

I used the time to work on my status and my future.

In these early years of the Cold War, the editorial line of the magazines that hired me wasn't working for me. Henry Luce, the head of *LIFE*, was a big advocate of the antired crusade.

Our negatives were the property of the magazines...

...and when they sold pictures to other publications, we got nothing.

I brought up the idea to friends, of starting an independent agency for photographers that we would manage like a cooperative.

And we would be free to choose our subjects.

New York, mid-April 1947, restaurant at the Museum of Modern Art.

Ok, Bob, so what do we call this agency?

My friends raise your glasses to the... MAGNUM agency!!!

We organized a lunch to baptize our new adventure that united me with Chim Seymour, Henri Cartier-Bresson, George Rodger, Bill Vandivert and Maria Eisner.

Moscow, July 1947.

Steinbeck's knee finally healed. Our Soviet odyssey started out badly. My numerous cases of photo equipment were stopped at customs.

The plainclothes policemen and cultural attachés were making things hard for us. I was not free to take whatever photos I liked. Some days my cameras were even confiscated.

For the first few weeks, I wasn't even allowed to take photos in public places.

This Stalinist ambiance affected my relationship with Steinbeck.

He accused me of hogging the books our hosts left for us in our rooms.

And of seriously monopolizing the bathroom like he had never seen.

Our airplane travels prevented us from any contact with everyday people.

The Soviets only showed us what they wanted to.

Only the extent of the destruction of Stalingrad and our freedom to walk around there gave us a semblance of a bit of truth.

Getting my film out of the country was a drama in its own right.

The Soviets wanted to develop it all themselves so they could control what would appear in the Western magazines.

On board the *Queen Elizabeth*, port of New York, February 1948.

Our book on the Soviet Union got a cool reception. But as a comeback, Steinbeck and I created a film production company called World Video.

I was certain that the new American medium, television, would give the press and its photographers a run for their money.

I was to shoot a series of shorts on Paris fashion, which was having a revival.

Sailing toward the Parisian studios of Christian Dior, Balmain or Jean Patou, I met a young fashion photographer, Richard Avedon, who gave me access to his address book filled with the contacts of wonderful models.

When I got to Paris, I set up at the Lancaster, and accompanied by famous models such as Suzy Parker and Bettina Graziani, I made the rounds of the fashion shows with my cameraman.

Alas, my luxurious lifestyle and my dizzying expense account justified the name of the project "Paris, Cavalcade of Fashion."

This financial exploit resulted in a long quarrel with Steinbeck and dear friendships with Suzy and Betina.

That escapade forced me to put away my custom-tailored, three-piece suits and don my battle dress again.

Off the coast of Haifa, May 1948.

Right after Illustrated and Regrads offered me the assignment, I jumped on the next boat to cover the birth of Israel.

I was to witness the fleets of Jewish refugees converge toward that oasis after years of suffering during the war.

The joy resulting from the creation of that nation was followed by the surprise attack from the Arab army. I am thrown back into combat with my cameras over my shoulder.

From camps of tents in Haifa to the pioneers of the kibbutz, I was there. Through my viewfinder, I captured all of it: the smiles of the new arrivals, the tenacity of the pioneers, the fierceness of the battles between the Jews and the Arabs in the alleys of Jerusalem.

I even witnessed the fratricide between Jewish militias during the Altalena passenger ship incident. I ended up carrying a scar on my thigh from a stray bullet.

I did not survive German shelling and Italian mortars to die there on that beach, betrayed by an Israeli bullet!

I went back there three times: in 1948, 1949 and 1950, and shot 700 rolls of stills, one film, The Journey, as well as an illustrated book with my friend Irwin Shaw.

Budapest, fall 1948.

After 17 years away, I returned to the Danube of my childhood. The towers of the Elizabeth Bridge stood dismembered in the middle of the river.

Holiday magazine asked me to shoot an essay on my native country.

My feet took me to the street in Pest, where my parents, Julia and Pezso Friedmann, had their apartment.

Endre! Get out of the bathroom!

Endre, sweetheart, I know that all these changes are hard...

Please, Endre, listen to your mother...

The tailors won't be using your room forever. We'll find a boutique soon.

Don't listen to neighborhood gossip.

Your father will be back from his European tour soon, and I promise that he hasn't thrown away our money in the Riviera.

Endre, open the goddamned door!

Nice, Henry Matisse's studio, August 1949.

Passing through the Côte d'Azur, I visited the master of Cimiez, who, surrounded by his band of cats, was preparing a chapel project. I had just left Picasso in Antibes, where I took pictures of his whole family. We talked about the good old days.

I was told Matisse was getting old. I found him quite alert, juggling with his charcoal at the end of a long bamboo stick. Like a real conductor!

The grace of his gestures and the simple hint of shapes, which he laid down on the rolls of paper stretched across his walls, hardly show up on film.

I took over the Paris office of the Magnum agency.

I had to force myself to play the role of administrator.

I did everything I could to find work for our penniless little group of photographers. Sometimes I even slept on the sofa in our office at 125 rue du Faubourg Saint-Honoré.

I had to find...

...the new star photographers.

I pulled in, in turn: Werner Bischof, Eve Arnold, Elliott Erwitt, Inge Morath and Marc Riboud.

I got them assignments throughout Europe.

My work was limited to well-paid essays for the glossies like *Holiday*.

That was a good thing because I continued to lose big at the table.

That resulted in arguments with Cartier-Bresson and Chim, who accused me of putting Magnum and its finances at risk.

I was not a very disciplined administrator. I often dipped into the coffers...

Paris, Bar des Theatres, fall 1953.

You are exactly my type of girl...

Your type at 500 francs, my dear...

I haunted all the main resort destinations of the nascent jet set, and I was loving being an unemployed wartime photographer. The Altalena bullet convinced me that whatever magical shield I'd had, that had allowed me to survive all the battlefields, had perhaps disappeared.

So, instead of the Korean War, I chose Paris' beautiful women.

My Paris routine was basic: sleep late in a room at the Lancaster or another such palace, inspect a pretty feminine back, daily bath, daily paper, come up with reportage ideas for Magnum, review racing news in any coffee shop, call the agency for ongoing business, light lunch, romantic rendezvous; end of afternoon: Longchamp, bar with friends passing through, gourmet dinner, poker or romantic evening, or both.

I'd just turned 40 and despite my hedonistic behavior I started to wonder...

What am I going to do for the rest of my life? Continue this circuit of assignments for *Holiday*, keep chasing money to cover my gambling debts, keep chasing women, without making any commitments?

The image of Capa was getting harder and harder to put on in the morning. And I saw a soft reflection of Gerda's face at the bottom of every glass...

An editor in Tokyo was waiting for me with a big assignment.

I flew to Asia at the beginning of April 1954.

Tokyo, April 1954.

I got a great welcome.

My assignment was a pretext for testing Nippon cameras.

I was given a brand-new Nikon that I used with color film.

I just walked around the city and focused on portraits of children.

I went from successful conferences to international dinners.

I received a telegram at my hotel from *LIFE*. I was to contact them urgently.

Their photographer covering the Indochina War had to return to the U.S. to bury his mother. *LIFE* offered me the gig for $2,000 a month, plus expenses.

I had just enough time to cover the Japanese workers demonstrating at the end of April before packing up my camera bag and heading to Bangkok. I was sorry to leave this photographer's paradise.

I arrived in Hanoi on May 9, 1954.

For the first time, I felt as though I had arrived after the fighting, that the mass had been said and that my photos would be passé.

The French army has just surrendered after the siege of Dien Bien Phu. All there was to put on film was the evacuation of the wounded and the prisoner exchanges.

Oh, the glorious return to the front of the great war photographer!

There were some that said I accepted this assignment for selfish reasons.

Although I was an American citizen, the U.S. administration had made my life difficult for the past year. I had a lot of trouble getting my passport renewed in 1953.

A report on me was sitting on J. Edgar Hoover's desk, and in this McCarthy era, I was suspected of being a member of the Communist Party. I had to justify my actions during the Spanish civil war, my friends and my work for Ce Soir and Regards. I had to renounce and explain it all in writing.

With my passport blocked, I couldn't leave France and I lost out on many assignments, most notably for *Holiday*; not to mention the loss of income. I had to mobilize my entire network of former high-ranking U.S. Army officials to fix the situation.

Some people thought that this assignment, favorable to the French army and published by *LIFE*, a notoriously anticommunist newspaper, could only improve my situation.

In short, 1953 was shit: my American headache, the agency's finances in the red, sciatica, chronic insomnia, exhaustion...

Tuesday, August 25, Indochina, south of the Red River Delta.

I accompanied a French brigade to this troubled area.

The objective was to patrol an open road between the villages of Nam Dinh and Thai Binh.

We exchanged fire with the Viet Minh several times. My shutter clicked incessantly. The delta fog haloed my pictures nicely.

Sometimes under far-off gunfire, sometimes mortar shells. We were constantly harassed by small groups of extremely mobile North Vietnamese troops.

Two English-language journalists were in my Jeep with me. I dodged oncoming trucks to get the best shot.

A squad walked into a dry rice field...

Quick! I'm on their heels. A tank opens the path while the bomb boys play with their frying pans...

The best angle is a slight overhang on the right. Quick. Run and climb the hill.

Quick! Take the shot before the guys move out of frame. CLICK. Again, you never know. Step to the side for a better —

Paris, Picture Services lab, June 1954.

Excerpt from General Rene Cogny's official report:
Photographer and American citizen Robert Capa died during an operation this Tuesday, May 25, 1954, near the village of Thai Binh.

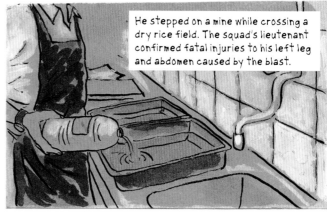

He stepped on a mine while crossing a dry rice field. The squad's lieutenant confirmed fatal injuries to his left leg and abdomen caused by the blast.

Evacuated by stretcher to Dong Qiui Thon under enemy fire, his death was declared by the military doctor of the base at 15:10 local time. His left hand was clenched around an intact Contax branded camera containing black-and-white film.

His effects also included a Nikon-branded device whose color film seemed to be viable. His remains were repatriated by C-47 plane to Hanoi, where he was given military honors by the Senegalese Guard.

During a short funeral ceremony the next day, I decorated the victim posthumously with the war cross, with laurels.

The usual condolences were addressed to the American Embassy, and the body was sent by plane to the United States.

His pale wooden casket was inscribed, in regulation black stencil:

Robert Capa, photographer.

Florent Silloray - Novembre 2015

The references I used to write this book are:

Richard Whelan
Robert Capa: A Biography
Winnipeg, Bison Books, 1994

Robert Capa, Richard Whelan
Juste un peu flou : Slightly out of Focus
Paris, Delpire, 2003

Alex Kershaw
Blood And Champagne: The Life And Times Of Robert Capa
Boston, Da Capo Press, 2004

Richard Whelan
Robert Capa, la collection
Londres, Phaidon, 2004

Cynthia Young
The Mexican Suitcase
Göttingen, Steidl, 2010

Sandrine Carneroli, Patricia d'Oreye
Robert Capa, un regard en avant
Gent, Snoeck, 2010

Bernard Lebrun, Michel Lefebvre, Bernard Matussière
Robert Capa, traces d'une légende
Paris, La Martinière, 2011

Cynthia Young
Capa in Color
New York, Prestel, 2014

I dedicate this work to VALERIE, who is the power behind this book.
It would not exist were it not for her continual support.

I want to warmly thank all those who have accompanied me during the roughly 40 months of this adventure, which I consider the result of a team effort. I want to thank Ms. Cynthia Young and the International Center of Photography in New York for their confidence in me, as well as for the freedom I was given for this project.

A warm thank you to the entire editorial staff at Casterman:

Charlotte Gallimard and Benoît Mouchart, who believed this book could happen. Vincent Petit, who supported me throughout this solo project, without putting pressure on me, and was the first person to read this book carefully and critically.

I commend the professionalism and incredible patience of Aloïs Duneau-Delis and Iris Munsch.

Thank you Nejib Belhadj Kacem and Nathalie Rocher,
as well as the studio team: Nicolas Vilet, Lydia Bierschwale.
Thanks to Kathy Degreef and Marie-Thérèse Vieira, who will help chart
this book's course.

Not forgetting the role Stanislas Gaudry and Guillaume Peyret played.

I also commend Guy Buhry's impeccable design work and lettering.

And what can I say about my printer with his magical touch and eagle eye? Patrick Freneau at ARCO IRIS worked hard to transcribe the nuances of the shades of ink and acrylic in the printing.

I know what this book owes to Jean-Michel Coblence.

Thanks to my workshop partner, Dan Christensen, for his sharp
eye and valuable advice.

Thanks to my children, Lou, Amélie and Cyprien, for their great patience and their hugs.

And finally, thanks to Christine, my mother, for her tender support.

Florent Silloray